STARTERS MATHS

Toyshop Maths

Macdonald Educational

Here is the toyshop.
The children are going to buy presents.
They will give the shopkeeper their money.
He will give them the change.

Can you see all the kinds of tops?
Some tops have to be whipped.
You push down the handle
on the humming top.
Watch the patterns when they spin.

Look at the sets of toys on the shelves.
How many dolls are in this set?
How many teddy bears are in this set?

Building bricks have different shapes.
We can arrange them in many ways.
Can you make some patterns with bricks?
Can you fit them back in their box?

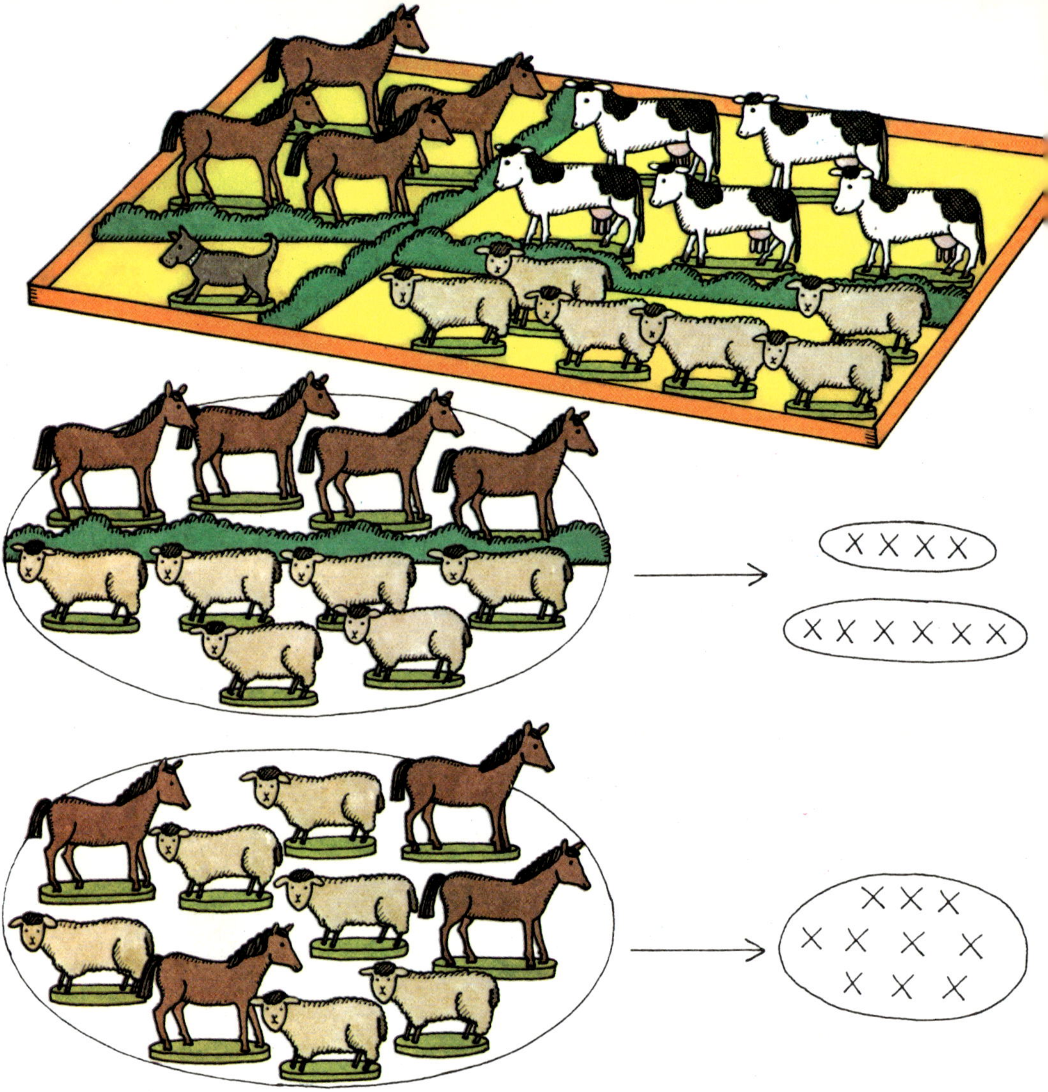

Here is a set of farmyard animals.
Count the horses and sheep.
How many animals is that?
Count the cows and horses and dog.

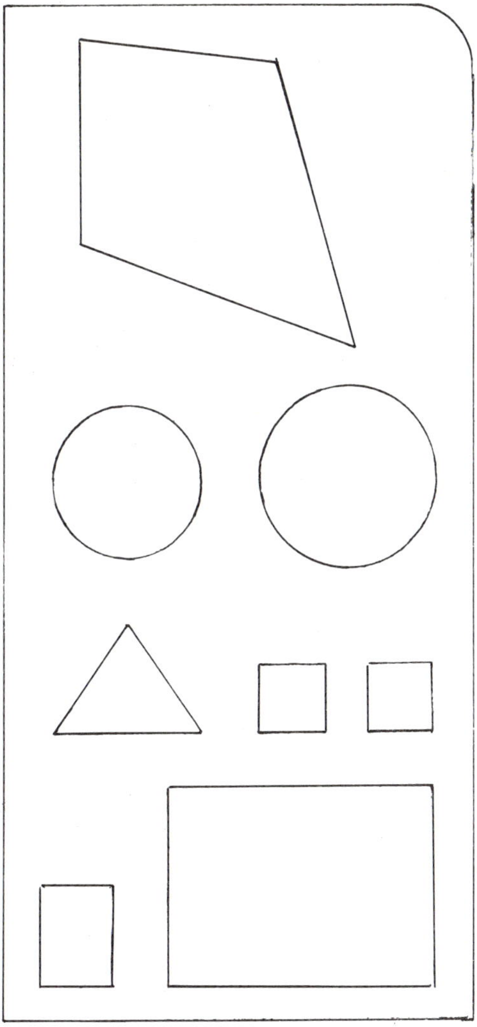

Here are some toys in the shop.
Look at their shapes.
What other shapes can you see
in the picture?

These children are playing with ropes.
Some children make patterns with them.
Which rope is shortest?
Which rope is longest?

All these toys move.
You wind up the spring on clockwork toys.
What do you wind on the aeroplane?
How does the Jack-in-the-box jump?

What do all these toys have?
How many wheels has the tricycle?
How many wheels do three tricycles have?
Would you put a balloon in this set?

These balloons are
different shapes and sizes.
Can you find the balloons with faces?
What would happen to the face
if you blew the balloon up more?

These children are playing shops.
They balance things on scales.
The boy finds how many apples
balance the sugar.
The girl finds the mass of the pears.

These children play with magnets.
The boys see who can pick up most pins.
The girls are playing a fishing game.
How many more than 5 is 8?

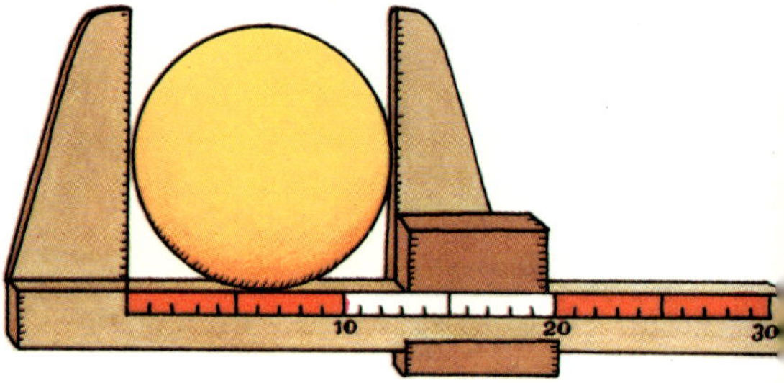

Here are some balls of many sizes.
Find the smallest ball.
Which is the largest ball?
How could you measure the size of a ball?

Here are some building bricks.
Do you know what shapes they are?
Model some of these shapes in clay.
Make your own patterns with bricks.

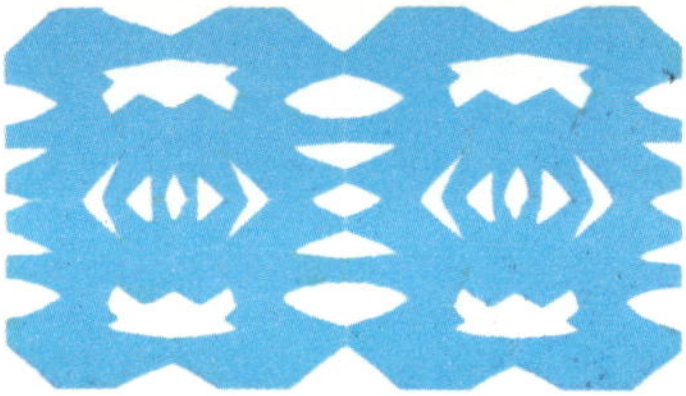

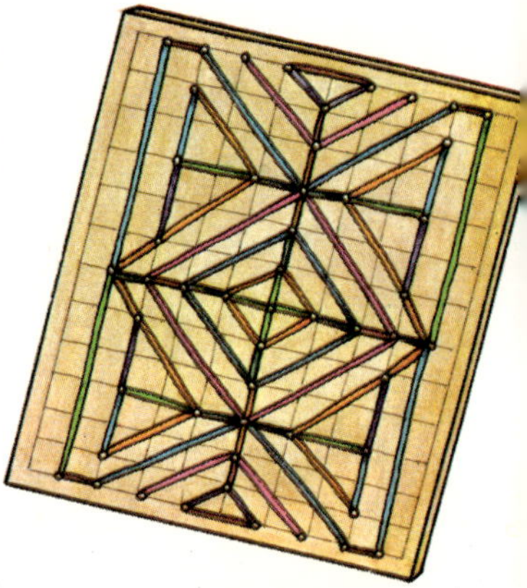

Here are all kinds of shapes.
Do you know their names?
Can you find a pattern
made with triangles?

Here is a set of dressing-up clothes.
They are in different sizes.
Do you know the size of your clothes?
What size do you take in shoes?

Toy rockets can fly to the ceiling.
Real rockets go far into space.
The rockets push the spacecraft
far away from the Earth.

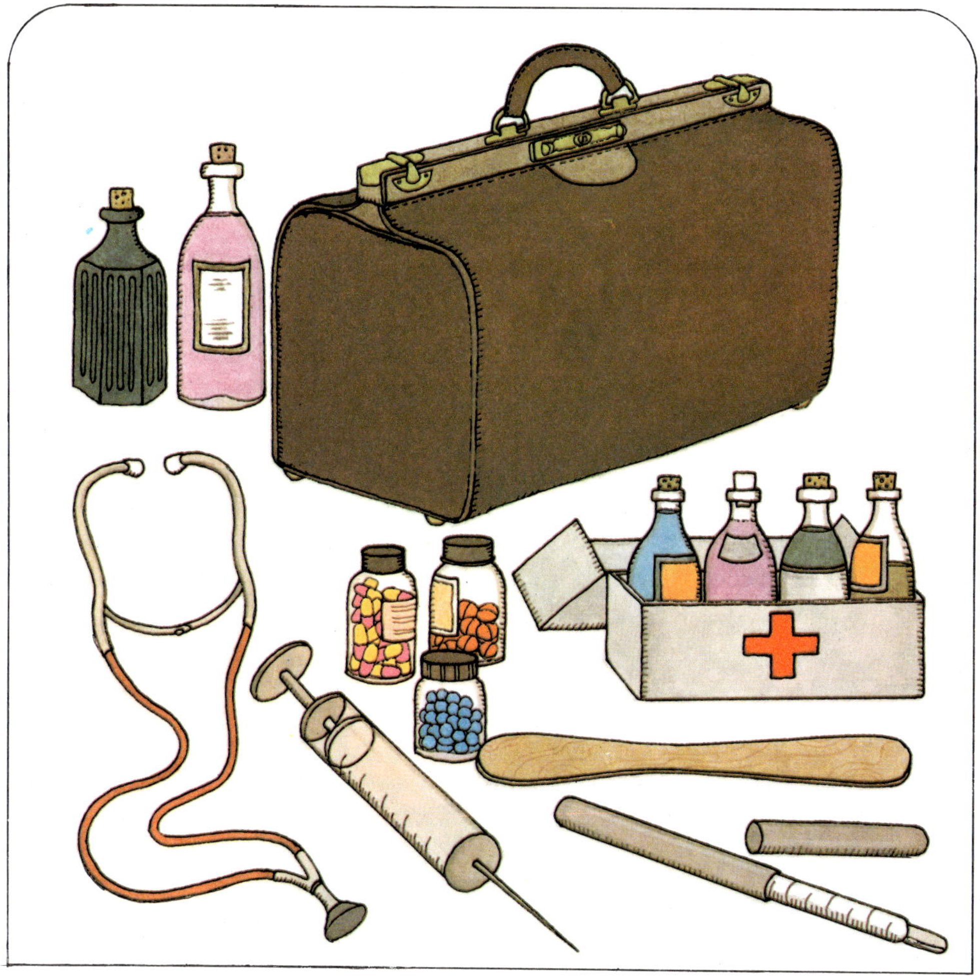

Who would use these things?
How many things are in this set?
Could you add anything to the set?

Which toy is the tallest?
Which is the shortest?
Is the cowboy taller than the Indian?
Do you know how tall you are?

The children are pushing and pulling their toys.
Which of the toys do they push?
Which ones would you pull?

Here is a set of racing cars.
Count the cars in the set.
What number is the red racing car?
Which two numbers add up to 9?

Can you find the longest pencil?
How many are longer than the blue one?
Can you see the thickest pencil?

Here are some musical instruments.
How many are there?
How many more would you need
to have a set of 20?

What shape is the toy crane lifting?
Try making your own shapes and models.
Triangles are strong shapes.
Use them in your models.

Can you see the numerals on the pages?
Which numerals are even?
Which numerals are odd?
How many even pages has this book?

Here are three toy mills.
What makes the water mill turn?
How do the sails on the other mills turn?

Index